Burying the Alleluia

New Women's Voices Series, No. 146

poems by

Nancy Susanna Breen

Finishing Line Press
Georgetown, Kentucky

Burying the Alleluia

New Women's Voices Series, No. 146

Copyright © 2019 by Nancy Susanna Breen
ISBN 978-1-63534-911-5 First Edition
All rights reserved under International and Pan-American Copyright Conventions. No part of this book may be reproduced in any manner whatsoever without written permission from the publisher, except in the case of brief quotations embodied in critical articles and reviews.

ACKNOWLEDGMENTS

Poems appeared in the following publications and online, sometimes in different form or with different titles:

The Atlanta Review: The Tease
Best of Ohio 1990, 2004, 2016 (Ohio Poetry Day prize anthologies): The Scavenger; When We Meet Again; Abandoned Stable
Black River Review: Roadhouse
Calyx: Mimosa Grove in Winter Wind
The Book of Donuts (anthology): Elegy for the Last Donut
Down the River (anthology): My Mother Swims
Encore—Prize Poems Anthology 2002 (National Federation of State Poetry Societies): Oblivious
fresh boiled peanuts: Fireball
Meridian: Princess Bride; Turnings
Pudding Magazine: Dunking Machine
South Coast Poetry Journal: Catherine

The following poems first appeared on the blog Nudged to Write (www.nudged2write.com) in slightly different form: Burying the Alleluia; Collecting Sheep; The Ecstasy and the Homicidal Rage; When Everything's the Matter

The following poems first appeared in 2009 "poem-a-day" comments on the blog Poetic Asides (www.writersdigest.com/editor-blogs/poetic-asides) in slightly different form: Dirty Cheaters; Never Give Your Troubles to a Monkey on a Rock; The Trouble with Catching Fireflies

Publisher: Leah Maines
Editor: Christen Kincaid
Cover Art: Nancy Susanna Breen
Author Photo: Lillian Westfelt
Cover Design: Leah Huete

Printed in the USA on acid-free paper.
Order online: www.finishinglinepress.com
  also available on amazon.com

Author inquiries and mail orders:
Finishing Line Press
P. O. Box 1626
Georgetown, Kentucky 40324
U. S. A.

Table of Contents

When Everything's the Matter 1

Abandoned Stable 2

Collecting Sheep 3

Mimosa Grove in Winter Wind 4

Catherine 5

Elegy for the Last Donut 6

Never Give Your Troubles to a Monkey on a Rock 7

Dirty Cheaters 8

My Mother Swims 9

Safe on the Bank 10

The Trouble with Catching Fireflies 11

Roadhouse 12

When We Meet Again 14

Princess Bride 15

The Tease 16

The Ecstasy and the Homicidal Rage 17

Instructions from the Good Witch 18

When You Wish 19

Fireball 20

Dunking Machine 21

The Scavenger 23

Oblivious 24

Turnings 25

Burying the Alleluia 26

*In loving memory of my mother,
Lillian Applegate Westfelt
1932-2018*

WHEN EVERYTHING'S THE MATTER

You don't have to read this.
In a world of earthquakes and riots,
dead piled on pyres, stores aflame,
in the midst of all that's burning,
these lines don't really matter.
I can describe the uplifting images—
a dog's joy at greeting his returned companion,
a hummingbird feeding her young,
a herd of sheep trotting down
a 19th century Cincinnati street—
they're pretty and appealing, but they don't
change the world. Although
for those few seconds I didn't think
about police shootings or Syria.
No one says absorption in the planet's crises
has to be 100%. I say a few moments
spent appreciating life's pleasures
make the tragedies endurable.
Is something the matter? Wait.
First, look at this.

ABANDONED STABLE

Three days before the Epiphany
and already the mangers are empty.
The plywood stables stand like
stage backdrops of failed plays
that closed out of town.
Beds of old straw, flattened
by New Year's rain, reveal
no evidence of the Family
who sought shelter and celebrated a birth.

O Wise Wanderers
in your crowns and robes, don't let
these lonely ruins dissuade you from stopping.
Pause long enough to revive
our dissipated joy
before you resume your search
for the MIA Savior.

January deserves to be as golden
and spicy as December, its gloom
brightened by the Star Without Borders
even as the electric stars blink off
in evergreens and along porch rails,
even as the jubilant hymns wane
in muffling bursts of mirthless snow.

COLLECTING SHEEP

Little lamb, who made thee?
Swiss woodcarvers, Mexican potters,
American craftspeople working in salt glaze.
There are plastic toys from a child's farm set
or a grandmother's button box,
and reproductions in the German style,
real wool over balsa bodies.

There must be twenty or more.
(Trying to count them for this poem
made me sleepy.) I'm not their shepherd,
but I provide them shelf space to graze,
safe from wolves and poachers, free
from the nips of border collies
bossing them into order.

They seem content, standing
or in repose. They gaze out at me
as if to say, "Be still. You, too,
could know this kind of peace."

MIMOSA GROVE IN WINTER WIND

They risk a ballet on a landscape
gray as a widow's vision.

Mad octogenarians, lithe and nude,
every gnarl protruding—
they are not ashamed

of crusty elbows, of skin
rough enough to bloody knuckles,
unabashed that their spines
creak in the frenzy,
that their limbs have forgotten grace.

They can dance. What dark staging,
such manic choreography:
They can dance, twisted women
with arms that defy their bodies
to brace them back.
They can dance. They know
how to throw their hair.

CATHERINE

You were the scandal of proper
Terrace Park: too open, too blonde,
your lust and lifestyle quagmired
in the congealed respectability
of the village. Your sudden death
by stroke at forty
seemed appeasement, the kind
of conservative act your neighbors
could acknowledge without chagrin.

You came to mind as I read
about the elephant buried
legs-up in some Terrace Park lawn,
at the former winter quarters
of Robinson's circus, where acrobats
shamed themselves with public tumbling
as the exotic menagerie paraded
through the staid residential streets.

Later I learned that you knew
all about it, could point out
the grand old house with the
moldy pachyderm under the lawn.
You, flamboyantly courageous
as a knife-thrower's target,
part fortune-teller, part trapeze queen
producing joy like gypsy silks
from your empty sleeves.

If you toe-danced back
along the silver thread
that separates our worlds,
I would not bore you
with the obvious questions.
I'd rub my hands to know
where the elephants are buried:
sanctimony, gray, cumbersome,
mocking us, belly up.

ELEGY FOR THE LAST DONUT

Pity the poor donut no one took
to avoid being the greedy pig
who grabbed the last one.
It languishes in its cardboard box
on the conference room table, gazing
hopefully through the cellophane lid
as the minutes tick away to quitting time.
If glazed, its glinting veil of sugared ice
melts into unappealing sweat.
If cream-filled, its delectable fluff
turns to spackle inside an old sponge.
If frosted, the coating hardens, then flakes
like whitewash from the walls of an aged shed.
Jelly remains jelly, but trapped
in a resisting disk of Styrofoam.
Someone might sneak a fragment, the remainder
lying like a dismembered limb
among a littering of colored sprinkles.
Even the cleaning crew can't be enticed
by a cinnamon twist completely undone,
denuded of sugar and spice,
its doughy litheness stiffened with age.

NEVER GIVE YOUR TROUBLES
TO A MONKEY ON A ROCK
for David Letterman

The monkey might handle things better
than you do, and then where would you be?
Troubles are like combs and drinking cups—
don't share them with anyone you don't know,
and that goes for monkeys, especially
the rock-bound kind. After all,

they're not known for their empathy
or their skill at resolving dilemmas.
They might turn troubles over and over,
try to crack them open or peel them;
or they might cast them into the water
like so many peanut shells,
then go chasing each other,
red-assed and shrieking,
up one rock and down the other,

and there you stand, no better off
than you were before, with the added
humiliation of having turned
to a monkey, God help us.
He has his rock.
He doesn't really care about
anyone or anything else.

DIRTY CHEATERS

"Clean your glasses!"
his mother told him
every morning. He pushed
them up his nose
until his lashes swept
the finger smears and water spots.

He'd washed them once:
soap, then a clear rinse.
The clarity was shattering.
He recoiled from the trash-
littered sidewalk, the large pores
on his teacher's nose, the bruises
on his mother's face and arms.

"I like them dirty," he said.
He preferred the scrim
of a thin film of dust,
or the fogging steam
of a cup of black coffee
that he sipped slowly,
pretending to be blind.

MY MOTHER SWIMS

The Ohio was all city river
where it rolled past the foot
of Gotham Place, the gasworks
upstream, the waterworks just down.
There my mother grew up,
nurturing no love for the river,
its lore and enticements.
She hated boats, hated fishing,
hated the floods that threatened
winter and spring. Occasionally
she went out on the bank
to watch and wave with the others
as the Island Queen churned
toward Coney's amusements and groves.
A few times she was persuaded
to go swimming, a rubber cap
over her hair, rubber slippers
to protect her tender feet
from booby traps of broken bottles,
raw bedsprings, and rusted tin.
She stepped reluctantly
into that dismal water, recoiling
from the smell like lighter fluid
and sun-bloated catch, lifting her face
from the unctuous, undulating rainbow
that rippled the current, slicking
the shore with a slimy mica sheen.
She never stayed in long, permeated
with the understanding of what filters are for,
the need to purify, what sinks
to the bottom, what floats to the top,
a film on her skin and the gasworks odor
still thick in the back of her mouth.

SAFE ON THE BANK

Two hours from home
on a cross-Atlantic flight.
I watched week-old CNN news
while waiting for the meal cart.
"Tragedy in Ohio" across the screen,
then a helicopter shot of a flooded river
and a gap between two familiar banks.
The anchor named the small town
near my mother's house. Two were dead,
others were missing.

It would be just like them
not to tell me, not wanting to ruin
my vacation. Or perhaps they all
were in the car when the small span collapsed.
My mind plunged into that current
to search the submerged debris
for loved ones. Hysteria rose past flood stage.

When I saw them in the airport, my mother
and sister, I gasped as if I'd finally
broken surface as I paddled toward them,
my feet touching bottom. Everyone
was fine, although my sister had crossed
the bridge just minutes before it went.
That was last week's news, though.
They were getting over it by now.

I, however, still trembled, still tasted panic
and muddy water. It would be awhile
before I could step back from the edge
of that broken bank, transfixed
by the thick, churning current
that concealed all the possible outcomes.

THE TROUBLE WITH CATCHING FIREFLIES

You think they're going to burn,
those blinking fluorescent
yellow-green butt bulbs.
Lightning bugs look like
floating embers from
the lady bug's house fire,
or the drifting sparks
from some cosmic craftsman
welding comets to the sky.

Once you enclose one
in your fist and realize
the coolness of fireflies,
you focus on the horribly
tiny movements tickling your skin.
This makes the inside
of your fist seem enormous,
bigger than the universe,
bigger than your imagination—

this living thing,
feet, wings, and fire,
all within your exquisite palm.

ROADHOUSE

I'm not a musician
but I can sing, let the band
fret over the particulars.
That bubbling in my throat
is a sweet, scalding vapor
I can't hold back—oooEEE!
I'm a steam whistle, baby,
and this shift's on!

Look at 'em dance, work-
grubby boys in feed caps
tapping heavy toes to a beat
they heard in their heads all day.
Even their women smile at me.
My rockabilly baby gnaws her rattle
in her playpen beside the bar.
She makes me safe. We've got that
in common, say the women's eyes,
softly searching mine
through the smoke. *Come on,*
they plead, *you've got
something to give that we need.*

So I go deep inside
where that wail starts in a woman,
that clenched muscle,
that shuddering hole full of
pent-up misery, or a joy so good
it can't cause nothing
but suspicion. I wrench it loose
with a wide-mouthed scream,
a mutiny, defying the limits of the melody.
I see them shake their heads, dazed,
clench their fingers. Some grin,
some got tears. Woozy with release,

they move their hands like clapping,
but there's no sound. Their men
holler, bop half-empty bottles
on the hardwood bar.

WHEN WE MEET AGAIN

You'll be dressed in one of your
square dance pretties,
flouncy yellow crinolines
poofing your full calico skirt.

I'll probably be barefoot, a child again,
in one of Grandpa's t-shirts
down to my ankles, my impromptu nightgown
when I slept on the living room cot,
cocoon-cozy in a fluffy blanket
with cobalt-dark blossoms
like stains of spilled ink.

You'll recount all that's happened
since you arrived over there,
the reunions and revelations.
As always, you'll hardly pause
for breath (if breathing
matters any more).
When I try to tell you
what you missed, the triumphs
and scandals, the weddings,
the grandkids you didn't meet,
you'll say, "Oh, I know already.
I was watching all along."

You'll add, "You cried too much.
I told you not to worry;
but, to be honest, I probably
would have felt bad if you didn't."

PRINCESS BRIDE

I saw her before they shooed me
out of the bedroom: Aunt Clara
sweating and struggling to breathe
within a tangle of damp bedclothes.

Grandma and the aunts—Grandma's sisters
and Clara's own—propped her up,
urged her to sip juice through a straw
despite her gaping mouth
and rattling gasps. Aunt Clara had sworn
she didn't want to live to be thirty.
Now, with her heart closing down,
she was escaping by weeks.

She'd always asked how
she would be dressed in her coffin.
"Like a bride," Grandma promised,
and spent too much on a real wedding gown.
"She looks just like Sleeping Beauty!"
Grandma said, trying to enchant me
as we entered the funeral home.

Aunt Clara did look elegant
but unfamiliar in the fitted white satin
that was so unlike the camp shirts she'd favored,
buttons gaping above her dumpy midriff
as she slumped and smoked. "Like

a princess," Grandma whispered.
But Aunt Clara looked smug in repose,
as if pleased with herself for not
living to be thirty, for not having to wake up
and sip juice, for getting herself a wedding gown
without Prince Charming bending toward her
with that kiss on his lips.

THE TEASE

Dawn was cast in no one's mold, none of this
wrestling with her conscience, her standards.
On slow numbers she gave the boys' shoulders
a luscious massage that turned them to Jell-O.

The censure in the chaperone's stare, the tsking
of good girls behind her back at the lavatory
mirror were irrelevant to her. She maintained
her cool glamor in the cracked-tile chamber
of mold smells and garish echoes, cleared the air

with a musk-scented cream, applied it
to her pulse points with a languid massage,
then stroked her mouth with passionate lipstick
a shade deeper than raspberry Jell-O.
When she swan-glided back onto the dance floor,
numbers of potential victims stepped forward

sacrificially. She nuzzled and whispered,
leaned into their shaving lotion auras
while her detractors floated like pastel
organdy clouds to settle in backseats,
behind bushes, protesting, wrestling,
mussing their hair, yanked about in a way
she would never allow as she controlled
each encounter with her sleepy, meaningful gaze

and gave so little of herself away.

THE ECSTASY AND THE HOMICIDAL RAGE

It's the same story, the same agony,
that feeling that overwhelms you,
with an ache you ignore
because you're so happy, so alive,
pain and ecstasy in every cell.

Try to concentrate. It's misery.
You have things to do, but all
you can manage is to lie on the floor
and daydream about him, damn him,
about the joy of breathing his air.

Then it ends, and it's the same
story, the same agony.
That feeling overwhelms you
with an ache you can't ignore.
You're so sorry to be alive,
pain and despair in every cell.

Try to concentrate. It compounds
the misery. You have things to do, but all
you can manage is to stare out the window
and slam your fist against your palm
as you daydream about
eviscerating him, damn him,
about the joy of cutting off his air.

But you'll do it again, you have to,
the same story, same agony.
You can't ignore the necessity
of that ache, pain and ecstasy,
despair and hope in every cell.

INSTRUCTIONS FROM THE GOOD WITCH

Click your heels and repeat,
"There's no place like home."

Click your heels and repeat,
"I'll never marry that badly again."

Click your heels and repeat,
"I'll never make the mistakes my parents did."

Click your heels and repeat,
"The government will protect us."

Click and repeat. It's all
in the repetition and the magic of three.
Jeweled slippers don't matter.
You can do it barefoot if you believe.

When you come to, don't be surprised
at the faces circling your bed.

Don't be surprised if you wake up
believing everything you say.

WHEN YOU WISH

Do not offer up your wishes to the stars.
Stars are all show, they're deceivers.
They care only about the light they send
and how far it has to travel.

They wheel above us, knowing
their elevation creates the impression
they have powers greater than ours.
They have seen the earthbound
lift their eyes to gaze the long distance.

In those eyes is hope, and a reverence
that makes the stars delighted
with their station in the hierarchy
of the heavens. They twinkle

with benevolence to attract
our love, which they covet.
*Look on us and state
your desires!* they sing,
preening in the dark sky,

glittering with promises
they know they'll never keep.

FIREBALL

"They're throwing fireworks at me,"
he frets at his first display, cowers
as if some giant lobs sizzling comets
from beyond the tree line and roller coasters.
Then he rallies as only a three-year-old
can, plants a stance in parched grass
to hurl imaginary rockets
into the face of the intimidating sky.

"I need one," he tells me.
"What color?" "Blue."
I pass the invisible missile,
spinning ball of chi
he grasps in cocksure palm.
Pitch perfectly timed—
an eruption of sparkly zigzags
quilts the smoke and moonlight.

We both rock back. His astounded eyes
ignite their own blaze, the delight
of unrealized power. After
the apocalyptic finale, our van snaking
through traffic, he still palms fireballs.
"I have two left," he confides.
"I'll throw them when we get home."
What a spectacle he must anticipate,

sky splattered with explosions
like a pyrotechnic spin painting.
The neighbors will run to gawk,
the big kids gape at his powers,
master of blast-off and flame.
Every dog on the block will bay
at the heavenly bodies he sends into orbit.
With skyward noses, they'll howl his praise.

DUNKING MACHINE

They're looking for games
and come to me, adolescent boys

who have fished too long in tubs
of tepid water where the fish

have numbered bellies
and the prize is always the same.

For a dollar I load their arms
with baseballs; there is no prize

but the pride of their aim
and the hilarity of dumping

my daughter into the tank.
She's about their age, and pretty.

They don't understand
what she makes them feel.

If she were a classmate,
they would probably pull her hair

and pick a fight. Sometimes
I get into it, too, done up

in oversized horn-rimmed glasses
and an enormous tie like their old man,

pouring on the paternal commentary:
You call that a throw, you sissy?

*Look at that pansy hairdo. Go ahead,
throw all night, you'll never*

amount to anything! That's when
they really buy up the balls,

taking turns at taking a shot,
the crowd rallying them on.

Every so often one of them will
connect. Sitting on the bottom

of the tank, I enjoy the fanfare
of their crying wild jubilation.

They go home massaging muscles
they never tested before.

THE SCAVENGER

The old man with the metal detector
could be an alien; the plate
of his detector hovers
above the grass like a spaceship.
He picks up signals through great
headphones. He could be
after more than lost change,
detecting where lovers fed
their passion to the clover,
their murmurs spilling like coins.
Melody vibrates along each blade
of grass, the sterling dirge
of snow melting, arpeggios
played by scuttling squirrels.
The old man hears it all,
salvages secrets others would crush
under their soles, unknowing.
He even pockets a stray nickel or two.

OBLIVIOUS
    Gettysburg, September 11, 2001

Summer celebrates its final days
on this scar-healed landscape.
Death does not intrude
despite the markers and monuments.
Mounted officers, infantrymen drawing a bead—
they dominate with resplendent elegance,
like statuary in a manor garden.
Thousands dead? It's hard

to imagine, gazing on a valley
where even restless spirits
may pause to reflect
on the benefits of eternal rest.
No blood on the boulders,
not today. Wheatfield, Peach Orchard,
Spangler's Spring—bucolic names
for nice places to linger.

In the Round Top woods,
shadows are pleasant, leaves
trace slow and graceful descents.
They soothe the mind
of imagined terror, mute the echoes
of shrieks and eruptions.
Not quite 9 a.m. Later,

the tour buses and vans,
the chatter of visitors about assaults,
strategy, the fallen.
Thousands dead?
It's hard to imagine,
the sky too pure and brilliant.

TURNINGS

At the moment autumn wanes
and winter begins, I pull
into the produce market. Here
spring brought johnny-jump-ups
like jewelry trays of amethyst and citrine.
Silver queen corn reigned the summer
in green husk robes, and hardy mums
and pumpkins enriched each other
all October, sunset orange against russet,
while cornstalks leaned
like weary, wise old men
musing on the seasons' turnings.

Today the market is barren,
not even a sprig of holly
or potpourri of fallen needles.
A sheet of black plastic barricades
the cases where Amish goods were sold.
Where peaches were sacked,
where carrots trailed lush greenery
and buxom tomatoes bulged
in plastic cartons, prim fruit baskets
pose with wax figurine perfection
within tinted shrink-wrap.

"CLOSED" signs close in
the register clerks, who labor grimly
to fill stacks of empty baskets.
They clutch at oranges,
apples, bananas with frantic hands
as if winter, newly arrived,
will shrivel fruit and faith
that this longest, darkest night
will give way to another growing season.

BURYING THE ALLELUIA

She wasn't a church-goer,
but she was joyfully devout,
praising the Lord in word and song,
even when she was alone. "Alleluia!"
was her salute, her prayer, her affirmation,
her cry of ecstasy and adulation
when the sun broke through the winter clouds
or she found her lost shoe behind the piano.

Yet, every Lenten season she buried
the Alleluia; not as a banner or special egg
she hid away until the Resurrection.
It was something only her soul
could conceal from her eager desire to jubilate.
It was a taxing sacrifice, more challenging
than anyone else's fast from chocolate
or a favorite television program.

On Easter morning, she allowed
consciousness to ease over her
like the soft light at a sunrise service.
"He is risen," she whispered. That
was the signal for the Alleluia
to come out of hiding, riding her voice
like a rocket of vocal fireworks,
an explosion of rapture that shot her

out of bed. "Alleluia!" she exulted
to the wet grass and the first buds of forsythia.
"Alleluia!" to the family climbing into the van
for church, to the hungover guy next door
padding out for his paper. "Alleluia!"
to the golden retriever passing by with her mistress,
to the person at the other end of every phone call
she answered the rest of that glorious day.

Nancy Susanna Breen is a poet, freelance writer, and editor. Her poetry has appeared in many publications, including *Atlanta Review*, *Meridian*, *The Book of Donuts*, and the prize anthologies for the Ohio Poetry Association and the National Federation of State Poetry Societies. Her chapbooks include *Rites & Observances* (Finishing Line Press) and *How Time Got Away* (Pudding House Publications). Her first chapbook, *Fake Slaps*, was a self-published collection of poems based on her experiences as a clown and former student of the Ringling Bros. & Barnum & Bailey Clown College.

She was editor of *Poet's Market* for Writer's Digest Books for seven editions; she also edited needlework and craft books as associate editor for Krause Publications and North Light Books. Nancy Susanna Breen's articles have appeared in *Writer's Digest, Writer's Market*, and *The Craft & Business of Writing*; one of her poems appears as an example in *The Practicing Poet: Writing Beyond the Basics* (Terrapin Books). She has served as screening or final judge for poetry competitions sponsored by Pennwriters, *Writer's Digest*, The National Federation of State Poetry Societies, and several individual state poetry associations.

An accomplished crafter and needleworker, Nancy designed and executed the embroidery on *Burying the Alleluia*'s cover. She blogs at www.nudged2write.com and resides in Loveland, Ohio.

www.ingramcontent.com/pod-product-compliance
Lightning Source LLC
LaVergne TN
LVHW021123080426
835510LV00021B/3304